S0-CAA-792

THE TITANIC

Virginia Loh-Hagan

45TH PARALLEL PRESS

Published in the United States of America by Cherry Lake Publishing Group
Ann Arbor, Michigan
www.cherrylakepublishing.com
Reading Adviser: Marla Conn, MS, Ed., Literacy specialist, Read-Ability, Inc.

Book Designer: Melinda Millward

Photo Credits: © Everett Historical/Shutterstock.com, cover, 1, 18, 22; © Everett Collection Inc / Alamy Stock Photo , 4; © XYZ/Shutterstock.com, 6; © volodyar/Shutterstock.com, 8; © nyiragongo /Adobe Stock, back cover, 10, 27; © Piccia Neri/Shutterstock.com, 12; © Andrea Izzotti/Shutterstock.com, 14; © Philcold/Dreamstime.com, 16; © Olga Popova/Shutterstock.com, 20; © North Wind Picture Archives / Alamy Stock Photo , 24; © Sven Bachstroem/Dreamstime.com, 28

Graphic Element Credits: © Milos Djapovic/Shutterstock.com, back cover, front cover; © cajoer/ Shutterstock.com, back cover, front cover, multiple interior pages; © GUSAK OLENA/Shutterstock.com, back cover, multiple interior pages; © Miloje/Shutterstock.com, front cover; © Rtstudio/Shutterstock. com, multiple interior pages; © Konstantin Nikiteev/Dreamstime.com, 29

Library of Congress Cataloging-in-Publication Data

Names: Loh-Hagan, Virginia, author.
Title: The Titanic / by Virginia Loh-Hagan.
Description: Ann Arbor, Michigan : Cherry Lake Publishing, 2021. | Series: Surviving history | Includes index.
Identifiers: LCCN 2020003319 (print) | LCCN 2020003320 (ebook) | ISBN 9781534169067 (hardcover) | ISBN 9781534170742 (paperback) | ISBN 9781534172586 (pdf) | ISBN 9781534174429 (ebook)
Subjects: LCSH: Titanic (Steamship)—Juvenile literature. | Shipwrecks—North Atlantic Ocean—Juvenile literature.
Classification: LCC G530.T6 L539 2021 (print) | LCC G530.T6 (ebook) | DDC 910.0163/4—dc23
LC record available at https://lccn.loc.gov/2020003319
LC ebook record available at https://lccn.loc.gov/2020003320

Printed in the United States of America
Corporate Graphics

TABLE OF CONTENTS

INTRODUCTION

About 23 of 885 crew members were women.

When it was built, the *Titanic* was the world's largest ship. It was supposed to be unsinkable. People thought nothing could sink it. The *Titanic* was built to last. It was super fancy. It was world-famous. It was the hottest ticket in town! Everybody wanted to travel on the *Titanic*. **Crew** members were excited to work on the ship. Crew are ship workers.

The **maiden voyage** was scheduled for April 10, 1912. A maiden voyage is a ship's first trip. There was a great party. Over 100,000 people came to see the ship sail off. There were many reporters.

The iceberg that sank the *Titanic* was approximately 100 feet
(30 meters) high and 400 feet (122 m) long.

On April 14, 1912, it hit an **iceberg**. An iceberg is a big, floating chunk of ice. The ship had received several warnings. But these warnings didn't get to the captain. The iceberg cut open the ship's side. Water flooded the ship. Nearly 3 hours later, the *Titanic* sank into the ocean.

The captain gave orders to load the lifeboats. There weren't enough lifeboats. The lifeboats also weren't filled all the way. There were over 2,200 people on board and only around 700 **survivors**. Survivors are people who live through a disaster. The sinking of the *Titanic* was one of the deadliest sea disasters in history.

FIRST OR LAST?

First-class passengers were given a music book with over 352 songs. Ship musicians could play any song on request.

There were different types of **passengers** on board the *Titanic*. Passengers are people who travel on ships.

The people who bought first-class tickets were very rich. Their rooms were at the top of the ship. They were fancy. They had windows. They had private bathrooms. They had big beds. First-class passengers had pools and ball courts. They also had many servants.

The people who bought second-class tickets were professionals. They were doctors and teachers. They had nice areas to relax. Examples are a library and a walking deck. The second-class rooms were comfortable. They had 2 to 4 beds. They were in the middle of the ship.

Third-class tickets were the cheapest tickets. These rooms were basic. They were at the bottom of the ship. About 10 people slept in each room. They had to share only 2 bathtubs.

QUESTION 1

Which ticket would you have bought? (The prices are based on today's U.S. money.)

A You bought a first-class ticket. This cost $1,700 for a single room. A **suite** cost up to $50,000. Suites are large rooms with bathrooms and bedrooms.

B You bought a second-class ticket. This cost $700.

C You bought a third-class ticket. This cost $170. Or you stowed away on board. **Stowaways** are people who don't buy tickets. They sneak on board.

In today's money, the Titanic cost over $100 million to build.

SURVIVOR BIOGRAPHY

Eliza Gladys "Millvina" Dean was born in 1912. She was born in England. When she died in 2009, she was the last surviving passenger of the *Titanic*. She was 2 months old when the ship sank. Her family set sail to **immigrate** to the United States. Immigrate is to move to another country. They were planning to move to Kansas. They got third-class tickets on the *Titanic*. Dean's father felt the iceberg hit. He told his wife to dress the children and go to the deck. Dean, her mother, and her brother escaped on Lifeboat 10. Dean's father died on the ship. His body was never found. Dean said, "We stayed in a hospital for 2 or 3 weeks for my mother to recover a little bit. And then we came back to England because we had nothing. We had no clothes. We had no money. And, of course, [my mother] was so broken-hearted. She just wanted to get home." Dean worked as a mapmaker and an assistant. She never married. She had no children. She refused to watch the film *Titanic*. She died at age 97. Her ashes were spread from the docks where the *Titanic* set sail.

TO HEED OR NOT TO HEED?

Binoculars are tools used to see far away. The binoculars on the *Titanic* were locked up. The crew member with the key was switched to another ship.

When the *Titanic* was sailing, there was more ice than usual in the area. Even passengers saw floating ice from the deck. There were warnings of icebergs on April 14, 1912. These messages didn't reach the *Titanic*.

On the day of the crash, Captain Edward Smith did get some warnings. He changed the ship's path. Ships reported several large icebergs in the *Titanic*'s path. But Smith didn't get these messages.

Lookouts work on ships. They work at the highest part of the ship. They look out for dangers. Hours before the iceberg hit, the *Titanic* was traveling at top speed. The ship's lookouts saw the iceberg. But it was too late. The *Titanic* couldn't turn fast enough.

QUESTION 2

Would you have **heeded** the iceberg warnings? Heed means to listen.

A You heard rumors of an iceberg. You heeded the warnings. You went to the top deck. You wanted to be close to the lifeboats.

B You believed the warnings of icebergs. But you waited for the captain's **evacuation** orders. Evacuation means to escape.

C You didn't heed the warnings. You believed the ship was unsinkable. You didn't think anything was wrong. You wanted to stay on schedule. You wanted the ship to keep moving.

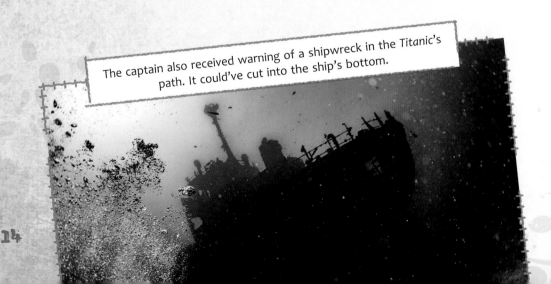

The captain also received warning of a shipwreck in the Titanic's path. It could've cut into the ship's bottom.

SURVIVAL BY THE NUMBERS

- It took 3 years and 3,000 workers to build the *Titanic*.
- The *Titanic* was 75 percent full when it set sail. It had room for about 1,100 more people.
- The *Titanic* sailed about 2,070 miles (3,331 kilometers) before it sank.
- About 60 minutes passed between the iceberg and the launch of the first lifeboat.
- About 490 passengers survived.
- About 200 crew members survived.
- Of the dogs on board, 3 of the 12 survived. Owners took the dogs aboard lifeboats.
- 242154 was believed to be the ticket number of a passenger who didn't set sail. This person got a full refund for their ticket before the ship left.
- The *Titanic* had 3,500 lifebelts and 48 life rings. These tools are good if you're drowning. But they won't protect you from freezing water.
- There were almost 400 iceberg **sightings** in April 1912. Sightings are reports of seeing something.

LIFEBOAT OR NOT?

The law required a boat the size of the *Titanic* to only carry 16 lifeboats.

Lifeboats are small boats. They can be launched from bigger ships. Their purpose is to **ferry** passengers to nearby rescue ships. Ferry means to carry from one place to another.

The *Titanic* could hold over 60 lifeboats. But the ship only held 20 lifeboats. They didn't want to **clutter** the deck. Clutter means to make a mess. Only half of the passengers could fit into the lifeboats. The lifeboats were on the highest deck of the *Titanic*. Only about 700 people made it into a lifeboat. Almost all of the lifeboats left with empty seats.

There should've been a lifeboat **drill** on April 14. Drill means a practice. But Captain Edward Smith canceled it so people could go to church. So, when Smith gave the actual evacuation order, people were confused.

QUESTION 3

Would you have gotten into a lifeboat?

A You stepped right into the lifeboat. You didn't think twice about it. You even helped row.

B You're not sure. When the first lifeboats were lowered, things on the ship were still calm. The lights were still on. People were still partying. The music was still playing. But you got in. You did this just in case.

C You didn't think the ship was sinking. You thought the evacuation call was a drill. You stayed inside. You didn't want to go out onto the freezing deck.

Lifeboat 7 was the first lifeboat to be launched. This happened at 12:40 a.m. An American silent film actress was on it.

SURVIVAL TIPS

Follow these tips to survive a sinking ship:

- Be prepared. Know where the emergency exits are. Know the evacuation paths. Find the closest lifeboat. Know where the lifejackets are.
- Listen for the captain's signal. When it's time to evacuate, the captain will sound the alarm. The alarm is 7 short horn blasts plus 1 long blast.
- Stay calm. Stay focused. Listen to instructions. Panic leads to pushing and shoving. This leads to injuries. Panic also leads to poor decisions. (Larger ships take longer to sink. So, take time to think clearly.)
- Large ships tilt. Hold on to handrails. Make your way to the top deck. Walk slowly. Avoid slipping.
- Follow the rats! Rats are the first to jump ship. The lowest parts of the ships are flooded first. This is where rats live.
- Feel the rolling of the ship. Ships roll with the waves. If a ship is stable, it could be filling up with water. A stable ship is a sinking ship.

WOMAN OR CHILD?

Captain Smith had served 40 years as a seaman.
The *Titanic* was the first crisis of his career.

Not everyone was let into the lifeboats. Crew members decided who got in or not. Those in lifeboats were more likely to survive.

Captain Edward Smith ordered his officers to put the "women and children in and lower away." Officers understood this differently. One officer thought this meant "women and children first." So, he let men in the lifeboats if there was room. Another officer thought this meant "women and children only." So, he didn't let men in the lifeboats at all.

"Women and children first" is a **code of conduct**. This is a set of rules for how to act. The idea is that women and children should be saved first. Another code is "The captain goes down with his ship." In the case of the *Titanic*, this was true. Smith sank with the ship. His last words are thought to be, "Well boys, do your best for the women and children. And look out for yourselves."

QUESTION 4

What were your chances of getting into a lifeboat?

A You were a woman. You were let on right away.

B You were a child. This includes people ages 14 and under. You were let on with your mother.

C You were a male over 14 years old. You were told to wait.

The longer people stayed on the Titanic, the less likely they were to live.

SURVIVAL TOOLS

The key to ocean survival is floating. Some of the most important tools are lifeboats and lifejackets. Lifeboats are light and sturdy. As such, they're made to move in rough seas. They can turn themselves the right way if they capsize. Capsize means to turn over. Lifejackets are filled with very light material, like foam. They displace water. Bodies already float. So, lifejackets don't need to support all of a person's weight. They just need to keep a person's head above water. They also keep people warm in cold water.

SINK OR SWIM?

Many people threw deck chairs and other things overboard.
They hoped to use them as floating tools.

People still on the *Titanic* sank with the ship. This included many crew members. They stayed behind to help people. They were the last to leave. Only about 23 percent of the crew members survived. For example, the ship's band had 8 members. They played on to calm the passengers. They went down with the ship.

Some people jumped off the ship. The water was freezing. Those in the water could only live for about 15 minutes. It was hard to swim in the ocean. The waters were cold and rough.

There was also a danger of being caught in the ship's **propellers**. Propellers are blades that spin. They help move ships.

QUESTION 5

When would you have jumped ship?

A You jumped off the ship right away. You swam to a rescue boat with an empty seat.

B You jumped off the ship as people started to panic. You found a floating object. You got out of the water. You waited to be rescued.

C You waited until the last moment to jump. You were in the water for over 15 minutes.

The *Titanic*'s deck was over 57 feet (17 m)
above the sea. This is a far jump.

SURVIVAL RESULTS

The *Titanic* was over 882 feet (269 m) long.
It weighed over 52,000 tons.

Would you have survived?

Find out! Add up your answers to the chapter questions. Did you have more **A**s, **B**s, or **C**s?

- If you had more **A**s, then you're a survivor! Congrats!

- If you had more **B**s, then you're on the edge. With some luck, you might have just made it.

- If you had more **C**s, then you wouldn't have survived.

Are you happy with your results? Did you have a tie? Sometimes fate is already decided for us. Follow the link below to our webpage. Scroll until you find the series name *Surviving History*. Click download. Print out the template. Follow the directions to create your own paper die. Read the book again. Roll the die to find your new answers. Did your fate change?

https://cherrylakepublishing.com/teaching_guides

DIGGING DEEPER: DID YOU KNOW...?

The sinking of the *Titanic* was tragic. Many lives were lost. Surviving history involves many different factors. Dig deeper. Consider some of the facts below.

QUESTION 1:

Which ticket would you have bought?

- About 61 percent of first-class passengers survived.
- About 42 percent of second-class passengers survived.
- About 24 percent of third-class passengers survived.

QUESTION 2:

Would you have heeded the iceberg warnings?

- The *Titanic* sank around the area called "Iceberg Alley." Ice is dangerous in this area.
- Ship captains order evacuations when there is clear and present danger.
- The *Titanic* was moving too fast. If the iceberg warnings had been heeded, the ship would've slowed down.

QUESTION 3:

Would you have gotten into a lifeboat?

- Those closer to the top deck were more likely to survive. This included first-class people.
- Crew members needed at least 30 minutes to lower all the lifeboats.
- About 70 percent of passengers panicked. This made it hard to get into the lifeboats.

QUESTION 4:

What were your chances of getting into a lifeboat?

- The survival rate for women was 74 percent.
- The survival rate for children was 52 percent.
- The survival rate for men was 20 percent.

QUESTION 5:

When would you have jumped ship?

- The *Titanic* snapped in 2 pieces. This happened before it sank.
- Women have 10 percent more body fat than men. This would help them survive a little bit longer in cold waters.
- After 15 minutes in freezing water, people freeze to death.

GLOSSARY

clutter (KLUHT-ur) to make a mess
code of conduct (KODE UHV KAHN-duhkt) a set of rules for how to act
crew (KROO) a person who works on a ship
drill (DRIL) a practice run
evacuation (ih-vak-yoo-AY-shun) escape
ferry (FER-ee) to transport from one place to another
heeded (HEED-id) listened to
iceberg (ISE-burg) big, floating chunks of ice
immigrate (IM-uh-grate) to move from a country to settle in another country
lookouts (LUK-outs) people who work on a ship and look out for dangers in the distance from the highest point on the ship

maiden voyage (MAY-din VOI-ij) a ship's very first trip
passengers (PAS-uhn-jurz) people who travel on ships
propellers (pruh-PEL-urz) spinning blades on a ship that help it move in water
sightings (SITE-ingz) reports of seeing something
stowaways (STOH-uh-wayz) people who sneak on board a ship without paying for a ticket
survivors (sur-VYE-vurz) people who live through a disaster
suite (SWEET) large room with bathroom and bedroom

LEARN MORE!

- Loh-Hagan, Virginia. *The Real Violet Jessop*. Ann Arbor, MI: Cherry Lake Publishing, 2019.
- Loh-Hagan, Virginia. *Women and Children First: Sinking of the* Titanic. Ann Arbor, MI: Cherry Lake Publishing, 2019.
- Sabol, Stephanie. *What Was the* Titanic? New York, NY: Penguin, 2018.
- Shoulders, Debbie, Michael Shoulders, and Gijsbert van Frankenhuyzen (illust.). *T Is for* Titanic: *A Titanic Alphabet*. Ann Arbor, MI: Sleeping Bear Press, 2011.
- Zullo, Allan. Titanic: *Young Survivors*. New York, NY: Scholastic, 2012.

INDEX

ABOUT THE AUTHOR

Dr. Virginia Loh-Hagan is an author, university professor, and former classroom teacher. She doesn't like cruises. She gets seasick. She lives in San Diego with her very tall husband and very naughty dogs. To learn more about her, visit www.virginialoh.com.